THE 100TH DAY OF SCHOOL

by Brendan Flynn

Cody Koala
An Imprint of Pop!
popbooksonline.com

abdobooks.com
Published by Pop!, a division of ABDO, PO Box 398166, Minneapolis, Minnesota 55439. Copyright © 2019 by POP, LLC. International copyrights reserved in all countries. No part of this book may be reproduced in any form without written permission from the publisher. Pop!™ is a trademark and logo of POP, LLC.

Printed in the United States of America, North Mankato, Minnesota

092018
012019

THIS BOOK CONTAINS RECYCLED MATERIALS

Cover Photo: Shutterstock Images
Interior Photos: Shutterstock Images, 1, 7, 10, 11, 15 (top), 15 (bottom left), 15 (bottom right), 17; iStockphoto, 5, 9, 12, 16, 19, 20

Editor: Meg Gaertner
Series Designer: Laura Mitchell

Library of Congress Control Number: 2018949958
Publisher's Cataloging-in-Publication Data
Names: Flynn, Brendan, author.
Title: The 100th day of school / by Brendan Flynn.
Other title: The hundredth day of school.
Description: Minneapolis, Minnesota : Pop!, 2019 | Series: Holidays | Includes online resources and index.
Identifiers: ISBN 9781532161957 (lib. bdg.) | ISBN 9781641855662 (pbk) | ISBN 9781532163012 (ebook)
Subjects: LCSH: Hundredth Day of School--Juvenile literature. | Holidays--Juvenile literature. | Elementary schools--Juvenile literature.
Classification: DDC 394.26--dc23

Hello! My name is

Cody Koala

Pop open this book and you'll find QR codes like this one, loaded with information, so you can learn even more!

Scan this code* and others like it while you read, or visit the website below to make this book pop.

popbooksonline.com/100-day-of-school

*Scanning QR codes requires a web-enabled smart device with a QR code reader app and a camera.

Table of Contents

Chapter 1

The 100th Day of School

Students sit in a classroom.

A **calendar** hangs on the

wall. The teacher adds

an X to one of the boxes.

The students cheer!

Watch a video here!

It is the 100th Day of School. Students and teachers celebrate. They have already learned so much together this school year.

The 100th Day of School usually falls near Valentine's Day in February.

Countdown

Mon	Tue	Wed	Thu	Fri	Sat	Sun
						1
~~2~~ 97	~~3~~ 98	~~4~~ 99	(5) 100!	6	7	8
9	10	11	12	13	14	15
16	17	18	19	20	21	22
23	24	25	26	27	28	

Counting Down

The **countdown** begins on the first day of school. Teachers plan activities to track the number of days. Different teachers count down in different ways.

Learn more here!

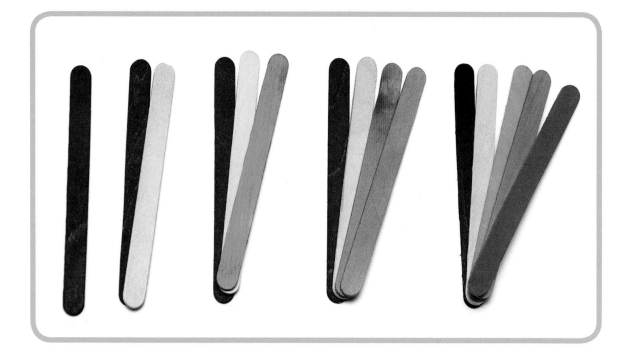

In one class, a student
adds a craft stick or a pencil
to a jar each day.

When there are 10 items,

the student wraps them

in a **bundle**. When there are

10 bundles, it is the 100th day.

In another class, the teacher puts a penny in a piggy bank. After 10 days, he trades the pennies for a dime. On the 100th day, the bank will hold one dollar.

This holiday helps teach students math skills.

Chapter 3

Making Collections

Students can bring items from home. They create their own collections of 100 things. They might collect 100 paper clips, 100 pencils, or 100 pebbles.

Learn more here!

Students place the
collections into plastic bags.
They write their names
on their bags.

Students can share their collections with the class.

The **metric system** is based on the number 100 and other multiples of 10.

Chapter 4

Celebrations

Some classes learn a new
song on this holiday. It might
be about the number 100.
It also could be about fun
things to do in school.

Complete an
activity here!

Students practice using the number 100. They celebrate completing 100 days of school. They celebrate how much they have learned.

Making Connections

Text-to-Self

Have you ever celebrated the 100th Day of School in your class? What did you do to celebrate?

Text-to-Text

Have you read any other books about holidays? What did you learn?

Text-to-World

One hundred pennies equals one dollar. How else do people use the number 100?

Glossary

bundle – a collection of things tied or wrapped together.

calendar – a chart that shows the days and months of a year.

countdown – the moments leading up to an important event.

dime – a unit of money that equals 10 cents.

dollar – a unit of money that equals 100 cents.

metric system – a system of measurement used in much of the world.

penny – a unit of money that equals one cent.

Index

Online Resources

popbooksonline.com

Thanks for reading this Cody Koala book!

Scan this code* and others like it in this book, or visit the website below to make this book pop!

popbooksonline.com/100-day-of-school

*Scanning QR codes requires a web-enabled smart device with a QR code reader app and a camera.